I've never felt like this before in my life.
What kind of ice cream is that?
Superman.
Maybe we should trick Daddy!
Can you write this one down? "I really like cobbler."
You guys aren't cool.
Someday I'll grow up and I'll know everything.
It's like I have a secret weapon inside me that makes me control my body.
How about we both be the boss?

KIDS ARE WEIRD

And Other Observations from Parenthood

Hello? Yes, Mommy's crazy.

BY JEFFREY BROWN

CHRONICLE BOOKS

SAN FRANCISCO

Thank you to Steve Mockus, Michael Morris, Marc Gerald, Emily Wismer, Gabby, Stuart, Izzy, and all my friends and family, especially Jennifer, Simon, and Oscar.

Thank you to Lady Pilot Letterpress for inspiring and printing the "Oscar" minicomic that became this book.

Library of Congress Cataloging-in-Publication Data

Brown, Jeffrey, 1975 –
  Kids are weird / by Jeffrey Brown.
    pages cm
  ISBN 978-1-4521-1870-3 (hardback)
1. Families--Comic books, strips, etc. 2. American wit and humor. 3. Graphic novels. 1. Title.
  PN 6727.B7575K53 2014
  741.5'973--dc23

                    2013030006

Manufactured in China

Written and drawn by Jeffrey Brown
Designed by Michael Morris
10 9 8 7 6 5 4 3 2
Chronicle Books LLC
680 Second Street
San Francisco, California 94107
www.chroniclebooks.com

WAITING FOR YOUR CHILD TO TALK REQUIRES PATIENCE.

What? What do you want?

BFFtoo PFTBB!

EVENTUALLY, THEY SAY THEIR FIRST WORDS...

Uh-oh!

Oscar, it's not "uh-oh" if you do it on purpose.

UNTIL THEY'RE TALKING! EVEN IF YOU CAN'T REALLY REASON WITH THEM.

Dad, you don't understand me. When I say "one," you just think "two."

IT'S A SMALL WINDOW FOR WHEN THEY SAY REALLY FUNNY THINGS.

You're not my best friend anymore.

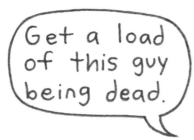

Get a load of this guy being dead.

They're having a how big they are contest.

Whoever's mouth opens wider gets to eat the other guy.

When I shoot fire, that's how I protect myself.

Tsschhhkkt!

See how I do that?

DREAM

Do you want to hear my dream?

Two cuckoo birds pushed me out of the nest!

Then I was flying on a pterodactyl!

And the pterodactyl ate the two cuckoo birds!

And then something happened.

I don't know what.

Someday when I've been Oscar for a long time, I'm going to turn into a baby.

And the other baby is going to turn into two Oscars.

There'll be three Oscars!

ABOUT SNAKES

Mating is like marrying, except some animals have live babies. Like humans.

This guy's sad because he doesn't get to have any love.

12:00 A.M.

This night is too long.

2:30 A.M.

Dad! Guess who's back?

5:00 A.M.

scuff scuff scuff

creeeeeakkkk

I climbed out of my bed and I said "hello."

GREMLINS Do you know what I would do if I were a Gremlin?

I would punch myself in the face, because I wouldn't want to do bad stuff.

SUPERMAN AND LOIS LANE

See that? She has a gun. She's a serious woman.

Instead of getting closer to my destiny, I keep getting farther away.

Oscar, will you unbutton me?

If there's any problem, you'll come ask, "What's going on here?"

And we'll say, "nothing, just playing."

BEFORE THE TIME OF THE DINOSAURS | TIME OF THE DINOSAURS | AFTER THE TIME OF THE DINOSAURS | TIME OF THE HUMANS

Mom, what's going to happen after the time of the humans?

What do you mean?

I mean, after humans die out, what's going to happen to the Earth?

Welll...that's why humans have babies.

Ohhhh, I see!

Who will be my Mom and Dad after you die?

PICTURE DAY

Tomorrow is picture day. Are you going to smile?

Yeah, I'm going to smile like this.

I have to wear a fancy shirt.

Did you want to button the top button?

You know why I wanted to button it like that?

Just for a more professional look.

I still don't want to wear a tie, though.

SIDEWALK CHALK

Look, Dad! I drew a bottle of wine!

Because you like wine!

SIBLINGS Oscar, do you think we should have another baby?

No.

Oscar, I think you'd like having a brother or sister...

Mommy has sisters... Uncle Doug and Uncle Steve are my brothers, and I liked growing up with them. I'm really happy that I have brothers!

Well, I don't see them living with us.

What should I be for Halloween?

A picture.

A picture of what?

And if any kid on our block needs something, I'll just go...

Wait, I'll get my stuff on--

and go do whatever they need.

phew

I've never felt like this before in my life.

My mouth and my mind just wanted to say all that stuff!

OSCAR
Enjoys long walks at the Field Museum, and eating macaroni and cheese

other books by JEFFREY BROWN from Chronicle Books

Vader's Little Princess
Darth Vader and Son
Cats Are Weird
Cat Getting Out Of A Bag

WWW.JEFFREYBROWNCOMICS.COM

My mouth and my mind just wanted to say all that stuff!
I don't like sleeping. It's boring. You just lie there and you don't even do anything.
Pretend you're watching a video of me getting eaten by a shark.
But not for real life.
Don't feel happy at me!
Do you want to hear my dream?
Let's go investigate that dinosaur!
I'm the Master of Bacon.
I don't have enough toys.
I miss Christmas.